Victoria Tonge '93

CARTOUCHES AND DECORATIVE SMALL FRAMES

Edited by

EDMUND V. GILLON, JR.

Dover Publications, Inc., New York

Published in Canada by General Publishing Company, Ltd., 30 Lesmill Road, Don Mills, Toronto, Ontario.
Published in the United Kingdom by Constable and Company, Ltd.

Cartouches and Decorative Small Frames is a new work, first published by Dover Publications, Inc., in 1975. The illustrations were selected from the sources listed on page 121.

DOVER *Pictorial Archive* SERIES

International Standard Book Number: 0-486-23122-4
Library of Congress Catalog Card Number: 74-15173

Manufactured in the United States of America
Dover Publications, Inc.
31 East 2nd Street
Mineola, N.Y. 11501

THE
PLATES

1

2

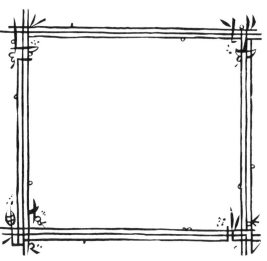

13

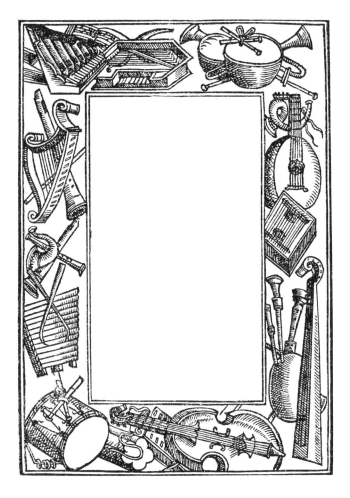

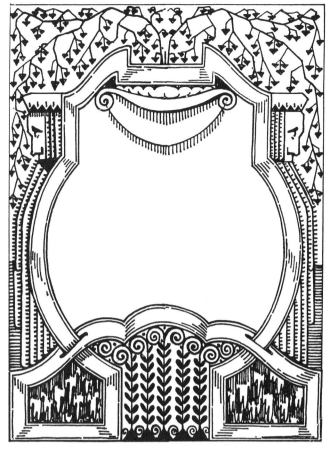

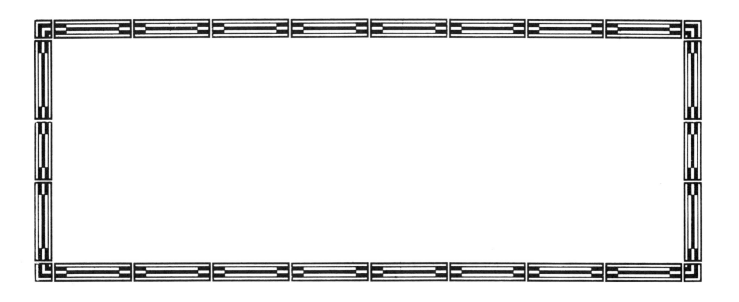

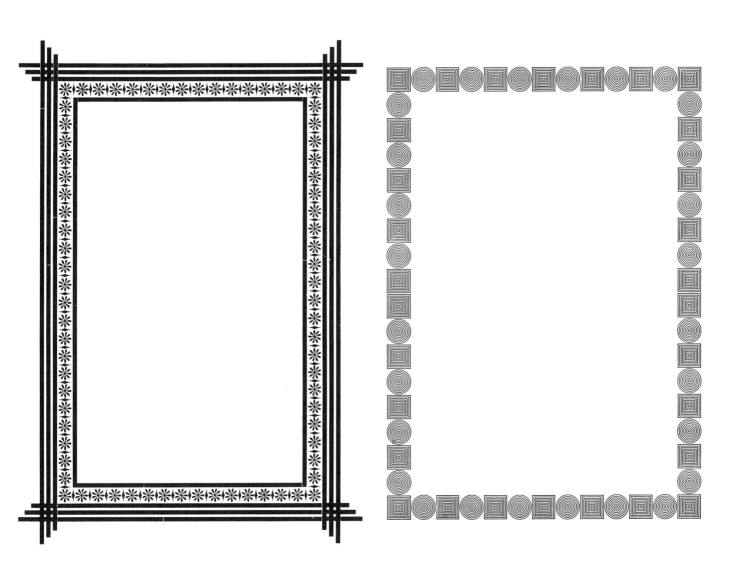

21

24

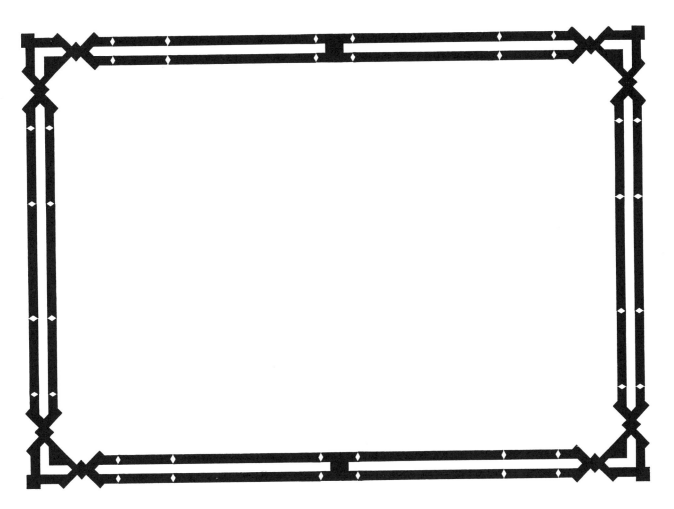

33

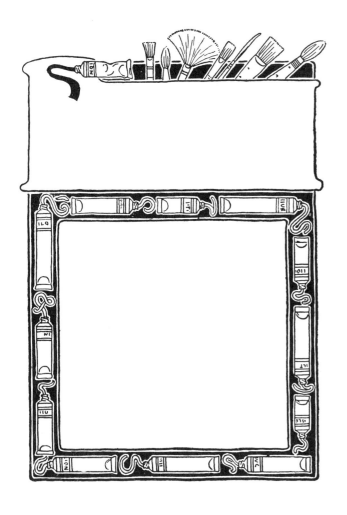

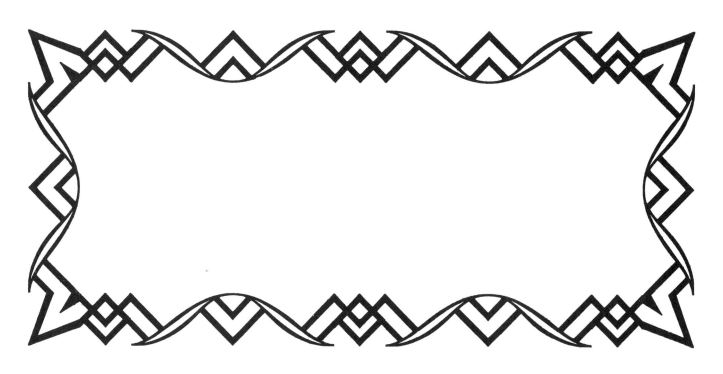

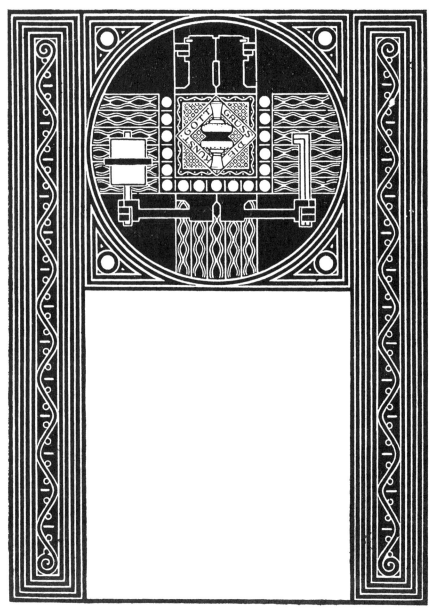

47

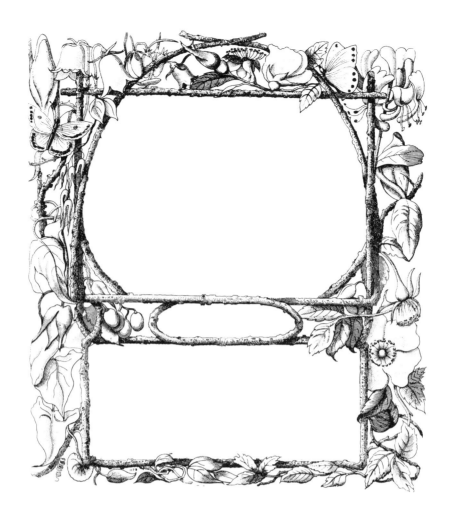

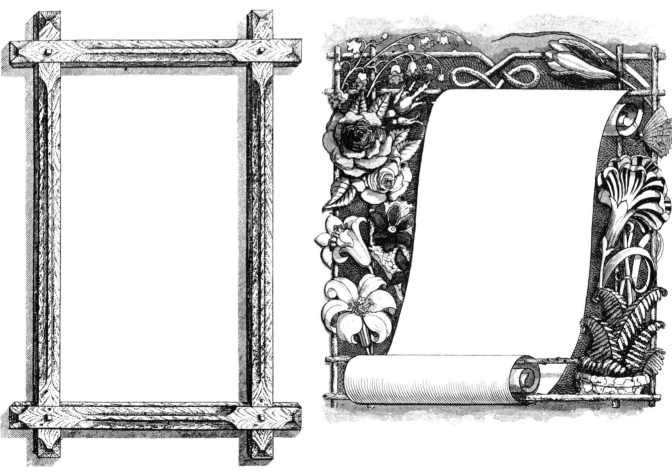

54

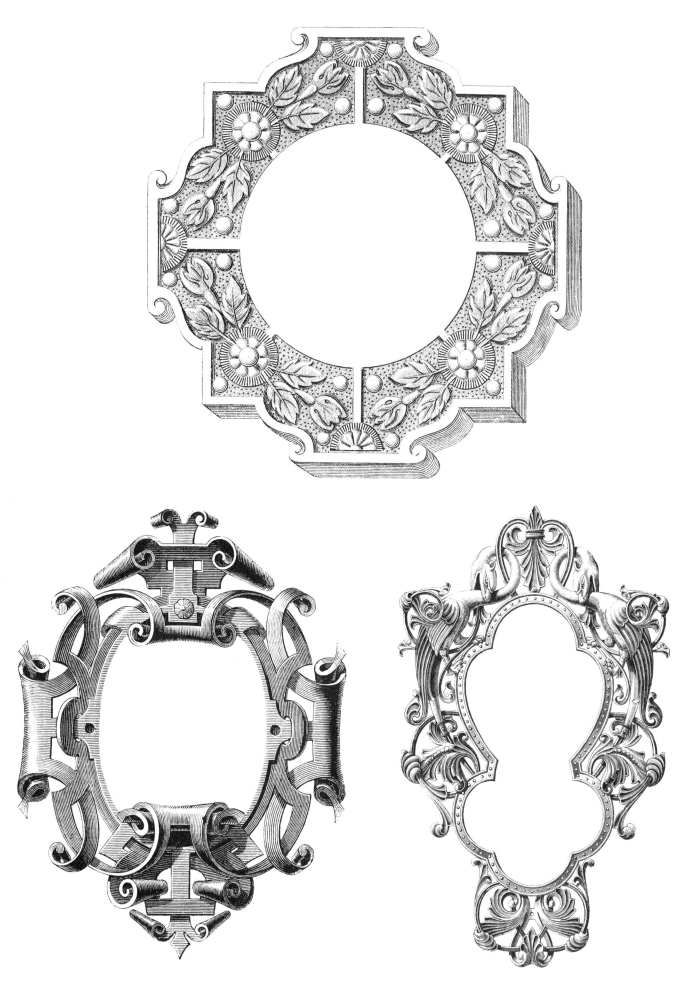

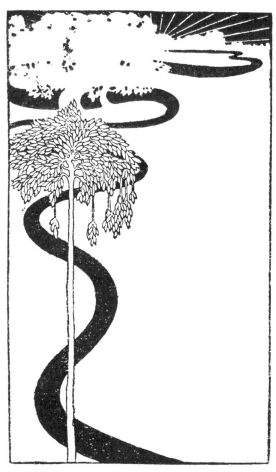

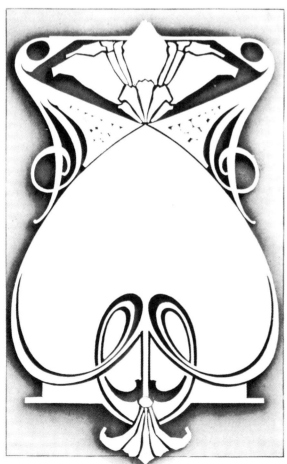

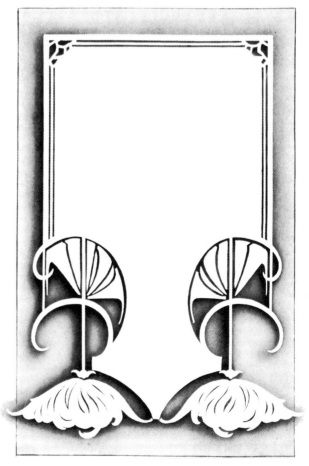

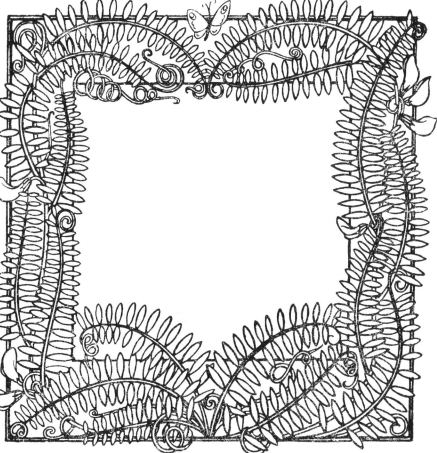

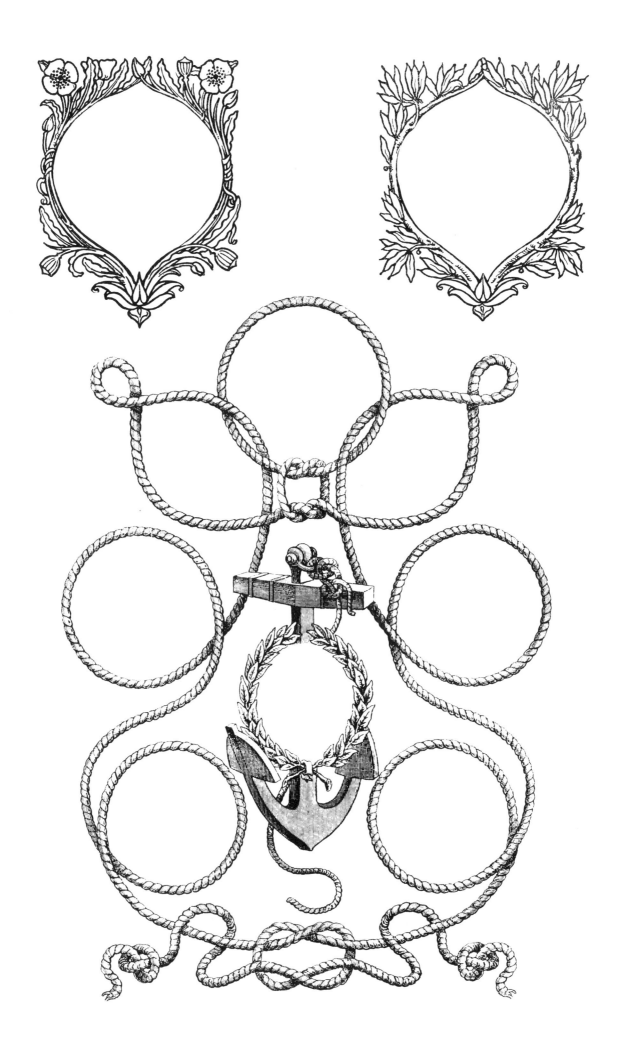

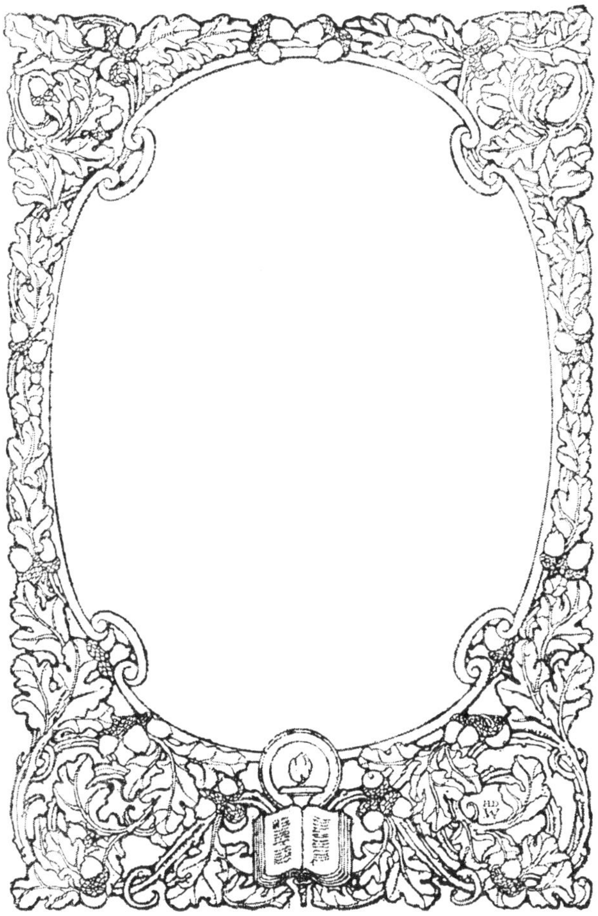

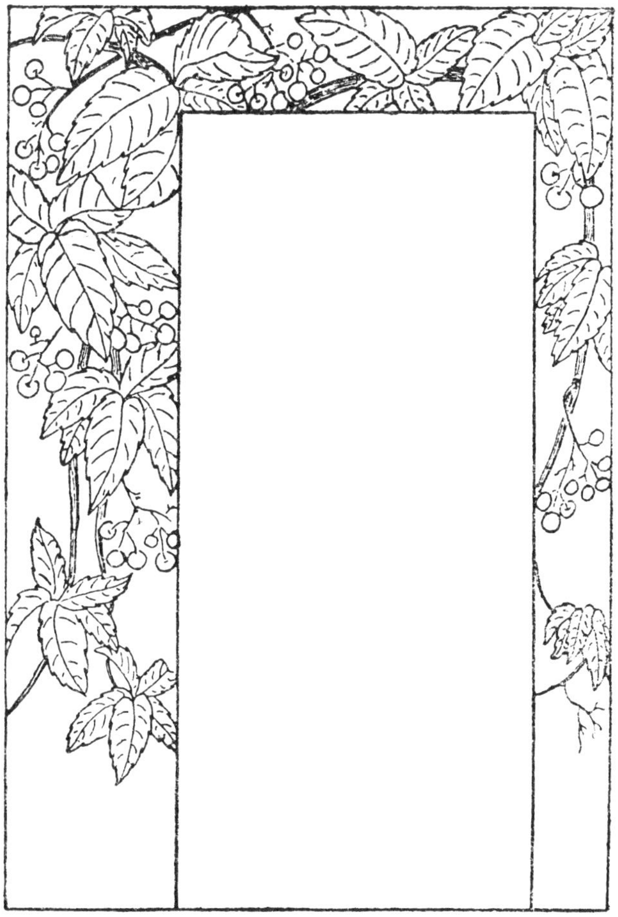

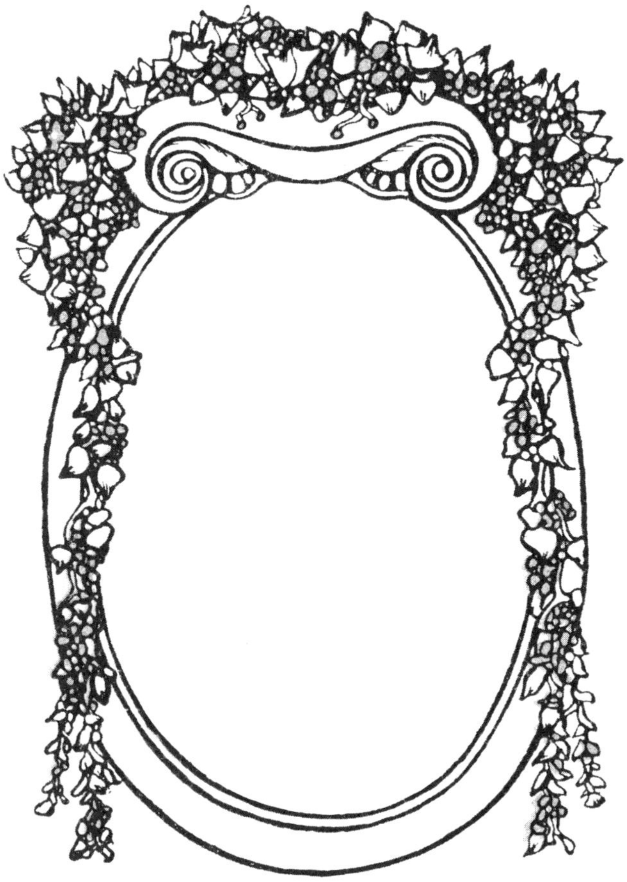

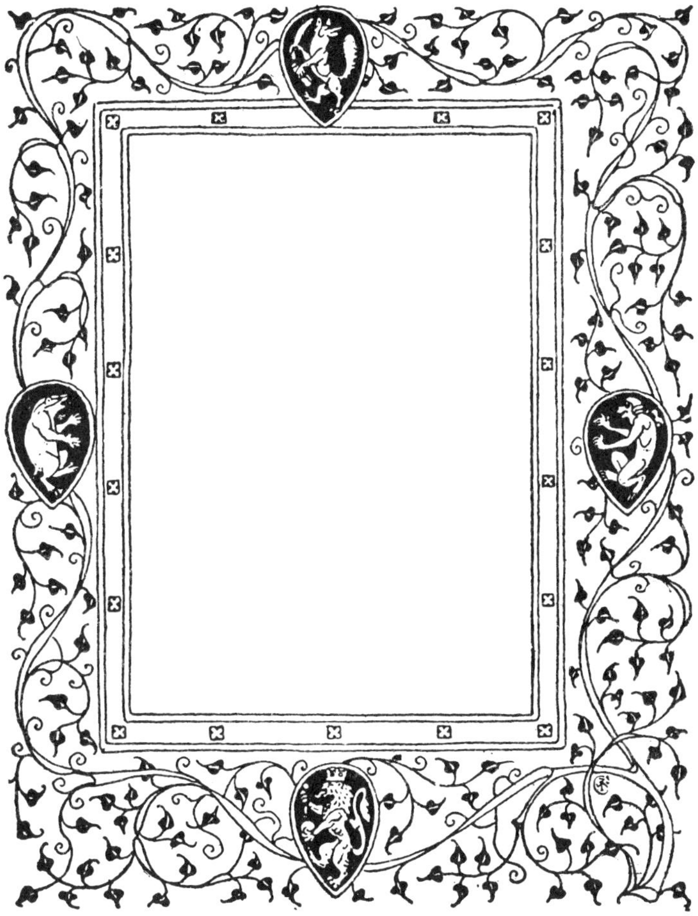

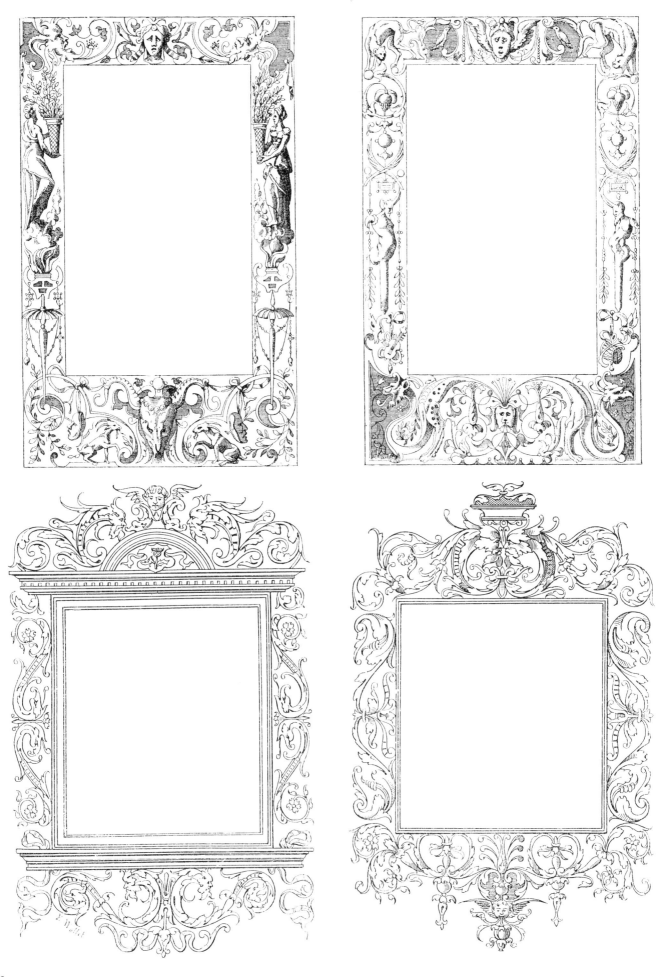

87

94

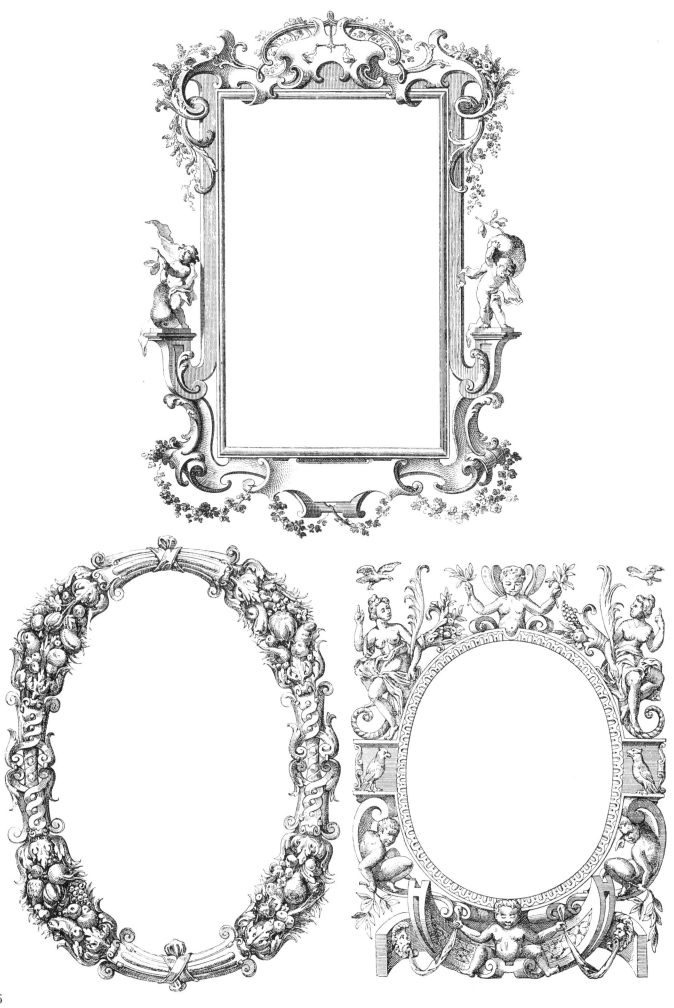

98

107

111

113

116

117

LIST OF SOURCES

THE ILLUSTRATIONS IN THIS COLLECTION WERE
SELECTED LARGELY FROM THE PUBLICATIONS LISTED BELOW.

Anaglypta. [A trade catalog of relief decorations, panelling, mouldings etc.] Darwen, England, *ca.* 1930.

Art et Décoration. Vol. XI. Paris: Emile Lévy, 1902.

Braungart, Richard. *Das Moderne Deutsche Gebrauchs-Exlibris.* München: Franz Hanfstaengl, 1922.

Catálogo de Tipos Maquinaria. New York· National Paper & Type Company, *ca.* 1915.

Claudin A. *Histoire de l'Imprimerie en France au XVe et au XVIe siècle.* 4 Vols. Paris: Imprimerie Nationale, 1900.

Collección de Xilografías Mallorquinas. 3 Vols. Palma de Mallorca: Imprenta de Guasp, 1950.

Crest & Monogram Album. London: William Lincoln, *ca.* 1890.

Fishenden, R. B. *The Penrose Annual.* Vol. 41. London: Lund Humphries, 1939.

General Brassfoundry: for Builders, Cabinet-makers, Bell-Hangers & Shipwrights. Birmingham: R. M. & S., *ca.* 1890.

Gerlach, Martin. *Gewerbe-Monogram.* Wien: M. Gerlach & Co., 1881.

Gerlach, Martin. *Karten und Vignetten.* Wien: Gerlach & Schenk, *ca.* 1910.

Knight, F. *Knight's Scroll Ornaments.* London: I. Williams and J. Griffiths, *ca.* 1840.

Leiningen-Westerburg, Count. *German Bookplates.* London: George Bell, 1901.

Ludwig & Mayer. *Schriftgiesserei.* Frankfurt a. Main, *ca.* 1870.

Maillard, Léon. *Les Menus et Programmes Illustrés.* Paris: G. Boudet, 1898.

Midolle, Jean. *Spécimen des Ecritures Modernes.* Strasbourg: Emile Simon Fils, 1835.

Monsen Type Manual. Chicago: Thormod Monsen & Son, Inc., 1929.

Ornamental Designs. London: Simpkin and Marshall, *ca.* 1860.

Ornemens Tirés des Quatre Ecoles [and subsequent titles in a series of volumes of engravings]. Paris: A. Morel, *ca.* 1845.

Pictorial National Library. [A monthly miscellany.] Boston: William Simonds, 1849.

Ratta, Cesare. *L'Arte del Libro e della Rivista.* 2 Vols. Bologna, 1927.

Ruscelli, Jeronimo. *Le Imprese Illustri.* Venice: Francesco de Franceschi Senesi, 1584.

Sauvegeot, Claude, and Reiber, Emile. *L'Art Pour Tous.* Paris: A. Morel, *ca.* 1870.

Schriftgiesserei. Frankfurt a. Main: D. Stempel, A. G., *ca.* 1910.

Seyler, Gustav A. *Illustriertes Handbuch der Ex-Libris-Kunde.* Berlin: J. A. Stargardt, 1895.

Shay, Felix. *Elbert Hubbard of East Aurora.* New York: Wm. H. Wise & Co., 1926.

Strong, Chas. J., and Strong, L. S. *Strong's Book of Designs.* Detroit: Detroit School of Lettering, 1910.

Thibaudeau, F. *La Lettre d'Imprimerie.* 2 Vols. Paris: Bureau de l'Edition, 1921.

Vander Cruycen, L. *Nouveau Livre de Desseins.* Paris, 1770.

Wenig, Bernhard. *Ex Libris.* Berlin: Fischer & Franke, 1902.

Zobeltitz, Hanns v. *Kulturgeschichtliche Monographien.* Vol. 4, Ex Libris (Bucheignerzeichen) von Walter von Zur Westen. Bielefeld & Leipzig: Velhagen & Klasing, 1909.